# Teesside
## and the Seaside

BRITAIN IN OLD PHOTOGRAPHS

# TEESSIDE
## AND THE SEASIDE

ERNIE CRUST

> *In memory of Jack Wright*

First published 2009

Reprinted 2009, 2010, 2011, 2012

The History Press
The Mill, Brimscombe Port
Stroud, Gloucestershire, GL5 2QG
www.thehistorypress.co.uk

© Ernie Crust, 2009

The right of Ernie Crust to be identified as the Author
of this work has been asserted in accordance with the
Copyrights, Designs and Patents Act 1988.

All rights reserved. No part of this book may be reprinted
or reproduced or utilised in any form or by any electronic,
mechanical or other means, now known or hereafter invented,
including photocopying and recording, or in any information
storage or retrieval system, without the permission in writing
from the Publishers.

British Library Cataloguing in Publication Data.
A catalogue record for this book is available from the British Library.

ISBN 978 0 7524 4731 5

Typesetting and origination by
The History Press
Printed in Great Britain

# CONTENTS

|   | Acknowledgements | 6 |
|---|---|---|
|   | Author's Note | 6 |
|   | Introduction | 7 |
| 1. | Industry & Shipping | 9 |
| 2. | Streets & Buildings | 19 |
| 3. | Shops & Businesses | 27 |
| 4. | Redcar for your Holidays! | 35 |
| 5. | People, Entertainment & Events | 63 |
| 6. | Schools & Sports | 107 |
| 7. | Redcar at War | 113 |

# ACKNOWLEDGEMENTS

First and foremost, my thanks to Alan and Julie Fearnley and the other relatives of the Wright family who kindly gave permission for me to compile the Jack Wright photographic collection into this book. My gratitude also goes to my old friend, Ian Denney, for giving me access to his father's photograph album. Thanks must also go to our local archives department, who have been very helpful on my many visits. To the following people who helped me with photographs and information, Hazel Thomas (*née* Lowe), Dennis Walker, Ken Bloomfield, Fred Firby, Adrian McTiernan, Cath and Tony Lynn, Phil Philo, the Jowsey family, Keith Burns, Jack Thornton, Stuart Wright, Janice Boon (*née* Playfoot), Wallace Holmes, the late Alf Kirby, Maureen Lowery, Max Clark, Ann Richardson, Michael Pacitto, Joyce Charlesworth, Vera Robinson, Dave Thompson, Dennis Beale, Andrea Kay, Charles Amer, Noreen Blackburn, Peter Warne, Wilf Parker, the late Derek Richardson, and not forgetting the many more who gave of their time to relate stories from the past.

# AUTHOR'S NOTE

The photographs in this book date from the 1930s to the 1950s and are from the Wright Collection and other personal photographs loaned to me. I have made no attempt to cover every town and aspect of Teesside life; the photographs selected have been my own personal choice.

# INTRODUCTION

Over the years many books have been written about Redcar, most of which have covered the town's long history concerning its connection with fishing and the iron and steel industries and with its development as a seaside holiday resort. This book looks at Redcar from the early 1930s to the late 1950s – and the nearby towns – through the lens of the camera of Jack Wright, who, through his profession as chief chemist, and later chief metallurgist, with Dorman Long Steel Ltd, had free access to indulge in his hobby at any of the Teesside works which he visited. This added immensely to his photographic portfolio.

I first met Jack in 1947, when I was fourteen, through my friendship with his son Jim, and along with several other of Jim's friends – namely Ian Denney and Jim Thomas – remained lifelong friends. As young boys we would sometimes go with Jim and his dad to motorsport events in the area, such as the Hartlepool Promenade Sprint, Airfield races at Croft, Scott Trials at Swainby, and of course Redcar Speed Trials on Coatham Sands, with Jack clicking away with his camera.

As I remember, this small group of friends became totally dedicated motorsport enthusiasts. I later learned that Jack photographed many other social events from the 1930s. When Jack died suddenly at home in the early 1960s, he left behind a rich legacy of photographs of importance to the history of the area and Redcar in particular. Forty years later I was offered, by Jim, the opportunity to use any of his father's photographs on motor racing when he heard I was publishing my two books on the photographic history of motorsport in Teesside, which I eagerly accepted in 2000. Sadly, only six years later saw the sudden death of Jim.

Happily, Jim's relatives have given me permission to use any of his photographs of social and historical interest. In some areas I have supplemented the book with additional images from local family connections, where I thought it of special importance to the social history of Redcar and beyond.

Ernie Crust

# 1

# INDUSTRY & SHIPPING

Keen local amateur photographer Jack Wright using his Exacta camera to make this self-portrait. A large majority of the photographs that appear in this book were taken using this camera. It was taken using a mirror, in 1935.

Dorman Long steel works, Middlesbrough, No.6 mill, finishing tram rails. The operator casually stands by as the red-hot rail rushes back and forth until it is of the correct gauge. The work was hard, hot, and at times, very dangerous.

Another view of No.6 mill, with the rail nearing completion before being cropped to size and sent to cool off. The rolling mills, Dorman Long Middlesbrough and Cleveland Works, supplied many hundreds of miles of rail and tram lines to be sent all over the world.

Newport coke ovens in the process of 'pushing', which took place every twelve minutes – the smoke, heat and heavy sulphur fumes pervaded the whole area, which at times made the nearby town rather unpleasant.

*Above:* Newport blast furnace works, Middlesbrough. Seen here is a furnace hand controlling the flow of molten iron into the pig-bed moulds. The workman on the right in the foreground is 'puddling' the molten iron to keep it flowing, and skimming off the slag.

*Left:* Tapping of a furnace at Warrenby was an everyday way of life for these furnace hands, watching the free flow of molten steel into the massive ladle, in 1936. The man in the foreground observes the flow through smoked glass. Even at this distance, the heat was tremendous.

Cannon Street was the main artery of the Newport Ward of Middlesbrough, a very close-knit community, housing most of the industrial labour workforce of Teesside. In 1935 times were hard, but people survived and helped one another. Looking east, the Transporter Bridge can be seen and, dominating the skyline, the giant gasometers, with the wording 'I am gas, use me' painted on the top. The one on the right states 'Gas – the modern fuel'.

Skinningrove Deepdale Ironworks specialised largely in rolling rails for London Northeast Railways. This photograph was taken in 1935 from the top of Skinningrove bank, hardly recognisable today.

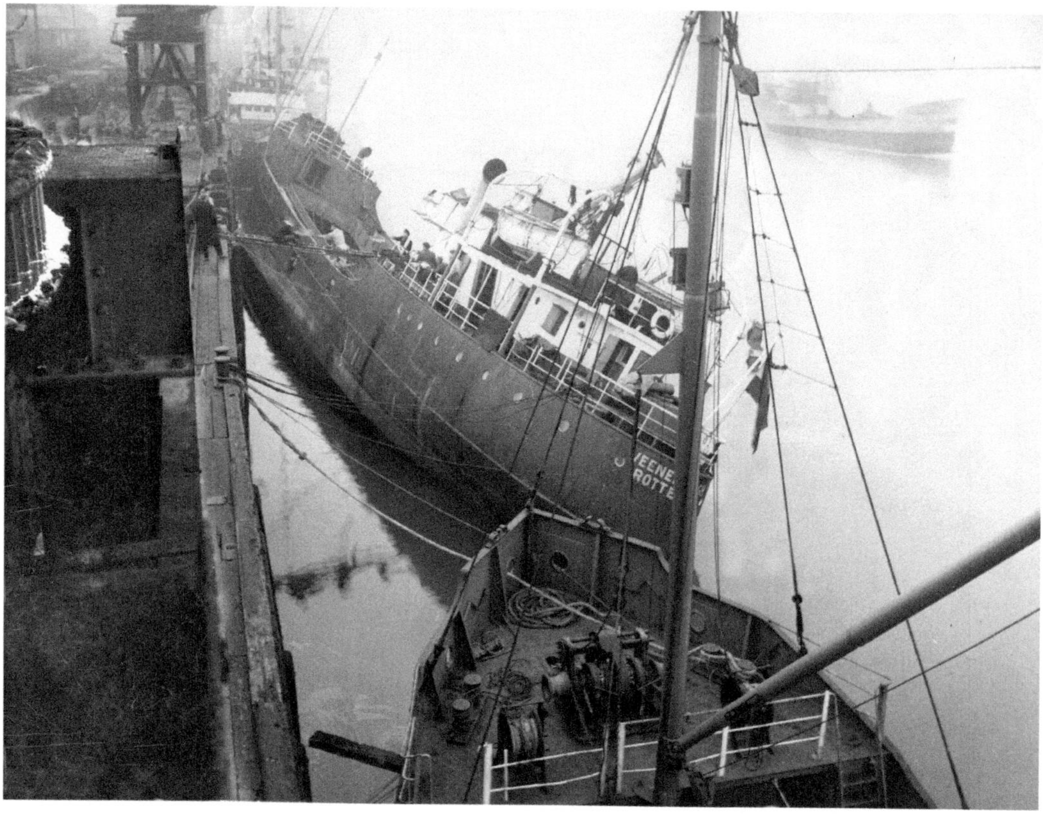

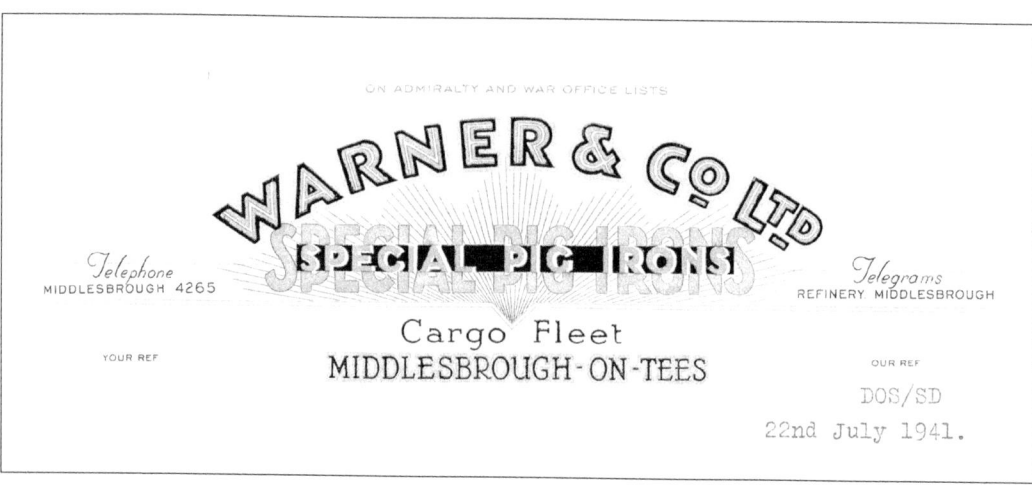

A weekly visitor to the Tees in the 1950s was the *Veenenburg Moller* from Rotterdam. The cargo could be anything from alcohol to butter – this photograph could have been taken at the Tyne Tees Dock or Dent Wharf. Although the ship is listing badly, this was not unusual in the loading process!

ON ADMIRALTY AND WAR OFFICE LISTS

WARNER & Co LTD

SPECIAL PIG IRONS

Telephone
MIDDLESBROUGH 4265

Telegrams
REFINERY MIDDLESBROUGH

Cargo Fleet
MIDDLESBROUGH-ON-TEES

YOUR REF

OUR REF
DOS/SD

22nd July 1941.

Warner's was one of the many specialist suppliers and exporters that made up Teesside's heavy industry. Such decorative letter-heading (this one embossed and in '3D') was not unusual at this time.

The SS *Hekla* at Newport Docks – one of the 'natural draft' type. The *Hekla* was nicknamed a 'woodbine funnel' ship, because of it's resemblance to the popular cigarette. It is seen here offloading scrap steel into the LMS and the NE Railways wagons, for the Dorman Long furnace. By the mid to late 1930s, industry started to emerge from the long Depression, bringing much more trade to the River Tees.

The 4,221-ton Greek merchant ship *Taxiarchis* ran aground in gale-force winds on Coatham Sands opposite the Coatham Hotel in January 1952. After several unsuccessful attempts to re-float her, it was decided to scrap the ship, and it was sold to Sheffield iron merchants, Thomas Ward Ltd. As with all other stranded ships at Redcar before her, the *Taxiarchis* was a huge tourist attraction. Coatham Hotel owner Charles Amer bought the cargo of timber from Lloyds, 40 tons total.

*Above:* The *Dunsley* ran aground at Redcar on 20 January 1946 – the crew refused to leave their ship when offered help by Redcar lifeboat. It appears that the *Dunsley* (built by Sunderland shipbuilders, Thompson's, in 1929) had an eventful working life. She was badly damaged by gunfire from the German U-boat U52 in 1940. The ship was then sold twice, after being driven ashore again. She survived until 1961, when she was sold to a shipwrecker in Italy.

*Left:* The SS *Athena Livinos*, driven ashore on Coatham Sands by gales on 28 February 1937. Just compare the size of the people and the lorry in the foreground to the size of the ship.

*Right:* Four-year-old Jim Wright stands for his father Jack, for a striking photograph of the giant propeller and rudder of the *Athena Livinos*.

*Below:* Looking downriver from Stockton, the Newport Road Bridge became the main road link between Yorkshire and county Durham. It was built in 1933 at the cost of £512, 353 by Dorman Long. It was officially opened to traffic on 2 February 1934 by their Royal Highnesses the Duke and Duchess of York, later to become King George VI and Queen Elizabeth.

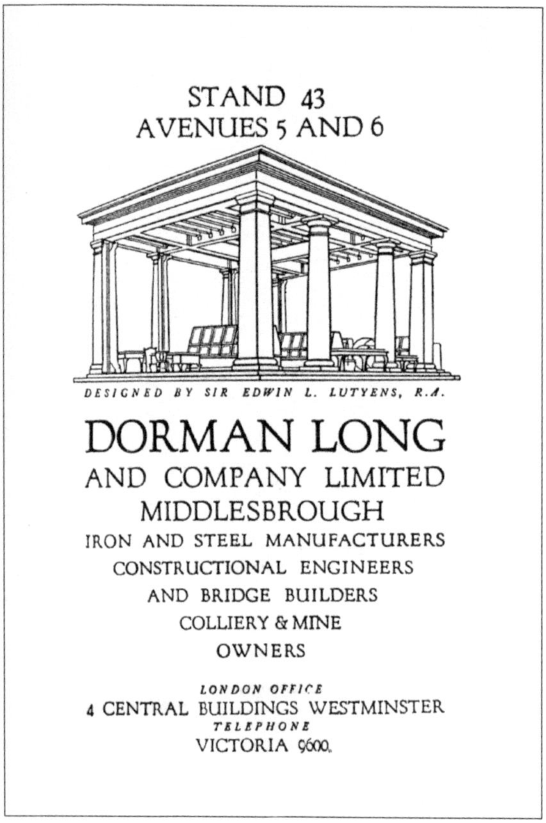

STAND 43
AVENUES 5 AND 6

DESIGNED BY SIR EDWIN L. LUTYENS, R.A.

# DORMAN LONG
## AND COMPANY LIMITED
## MIDDLESBROUGH
IRON AND STEEL MANUFACTURERS
CONSTRUCTIONAL ENGINEERS
AND BRIDGE BUILDERS
COLLIERY & MINE
OWNERS

LONDON OFFICE
4 CENTRAL BUILDINGS WESTMINSTER
TELEPHONE
VICTORIA 9600.

*Above:* Approaching the Newport Bridge from the Middlesbrough Yorkshire side of the river, the very new-looking roundabout, with a conspicuous lack of traffic in 1934. The enormous bridge-lifting gear dwarfs the nearby houses. Note the Newport post office on the left – today unrecognisable with the A66 flyover.

*Left:* World famous for its bridge-building, by the 1930s Dorman Long Steel Ltd, Middlesbrough, had expanded into structural engineering. Redcar works concentrated on rolling steel plates, Cleveland works on light sections and bar, and Middlesbrough produced heavy semi-finished stock.

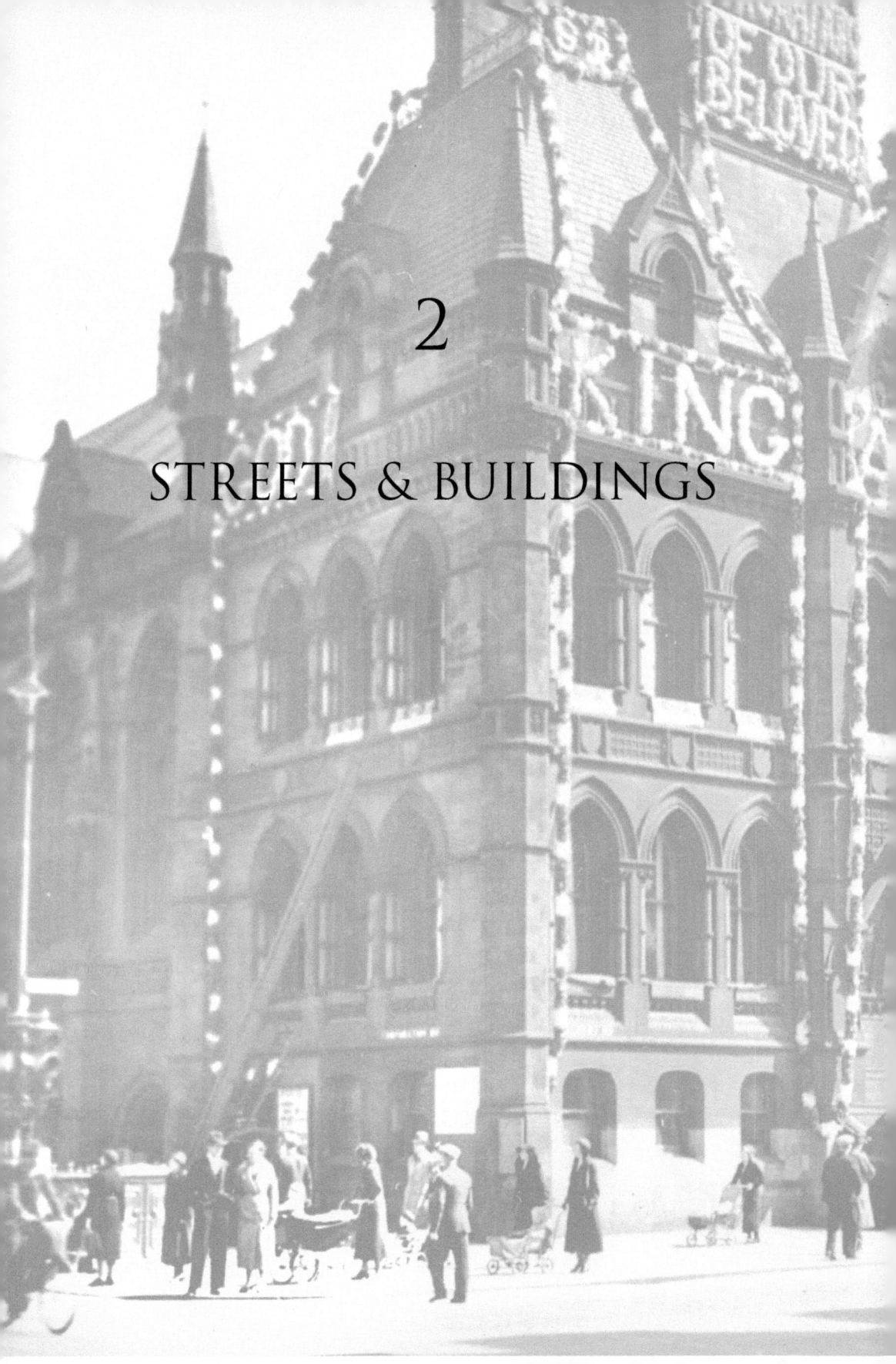

# 2
# STREETS & BUILDINGS

*Above:* The coronation of King George VI and Queen Elizabeth in May 1937 was a huge event throughout the country – Teesside as a whole played its part, with special events for all age groups. The children in particular were well-catered for with sports and street parties – the streets were judged and prizes given for the best decorated.

*Left:* Work in progress: decorating the Middlesbrough Town Hall on a sunny day in May 1937. Disappointingly, it all looked most dismal on the day of the celebrations. The mothers with children in the varied styles of pram are noteworthy. Little has changed today, except that there are no longer any underground toilets near the traffic lights, and part of Corporation Road is now pedestrianised.

A familiar figure in the streets of Teesside in the 1920s and '30s, Tommy West, the scissor-grinder, epitomises the working-class area of Middlesbrough, seen here in Wilson Street. The backdrop of billboard advertising on gable ends of streets was commonplace. The ever-popular Frank E. Franks variety shows at the Empire Theatre were legendary. The 'Battleaxe' tobacco was for pipe smokers, and was likened to smoking tarry rope! The World Speedway Championship at Cleveland Park Stadium starred some familiar names.

Looking down Linthorpe Road, Middlesbrough from Devonshire Road/Cumberland Road in 1934. To the left is the well-known Rowland Wynn garage, which was Middlesbrough's Chrysler agency. Boots the chemist is next door but one, and on the left in the far distance the dome of the Wesley Chapel, built in 1871, can be seen.

The street decorations are completed – some of the hardworking mothers of the streets in the Newport Cannon Street area of Middlesbrough can now take a break before the street party begins!

Redcar High Street in 1953 – the site of the weekly market. Patterson's sweetshop can be seen to the right of the picture. The doorway next to the shop is the old passageway through to Lord Street, known as Jerusalem passage. Note Suttill's tripe shop on the left, next to the fancy goods and brassware shop. Most of this block was demolished for the new Louis Playfoot car showroom and petrol station in 1959.

A view 200 yards down the High Street from the preceding picture. The horse and cart on the left, standing in front of the old Drill Hall, are looking towards the town. With only two motor vehicles, it gives us a reminder of how quiet and uncluttered the town was in the late 1920s and early '30s. Today from this point westwards, the High Street is pedestrianised.

Louis Playfoot's new High Street garage, Redcar, by night. In the late 1950s new cars are becoming more plentiful and petrol was no longer on ration, except for a short period during the Suez Crisis. Louis' new garage held the Vauxhall agency.

The original road from Middlesbrough to Redcar and Saltburn, before the trunk road opened, was through the village of Eston, with the backdrop of the Eston Hills. It presents a quiet scene in 1937. This bus drop-off point was a good start to the country walk up to the top of Eston Nab for a fantastic view of Teesside. Note the First World War memorial.

Middlesbrough town shopping centre. The double-fronted shop of the Scotch Wool Shop is sited on the corner of Fallows Street and Linthorpe Road, while opposite is Spark's, the well-known confectioners and café. The entrance to the upstairs café can be seen in Newport Crescent side street.

Late-night opening at Newhouse Department Store and Burton's the Tailor's in the 1930s. Situated in the heart of Middlesbrough town centre at the crossroads of Linthorpe, Newport and Corporation Roads, with poor street lighting, the shops provided a warm welcome on what appears to be a cold, wet evening.

Next to the Coatham Hotel at the west end of the Promenade, the low wooden building known as the Palais de Dance had several changes of use over the years including; dancing, roller skating rink, boxing exhibitions and amusements. The world-record car, the Sunbeam Silver Bullet, was once displayed here.

Middlesbrough railway station in 1937, decorated for the coronation of King George VI. Ponder a while with a magnifying glass and absorb the splendour of this magnificent example of architectural engineering. Sadly, only five years later in 1942, two German bombs ripped through this beautiful arched steel and glass dome, killing eight people and injuring a further fifty-six.

A view from the other side of the station, looking towards Redcar and Saltburn. Following the air raid of August 1942, the station was up and running in a very short time – however it was never rebuilt to its former Victorian splendour.

# 3
# SHOPS & BUSINESSES

# LATEST FASHIONS AT ROBINA BROWN'S.

L. AISBETT - I. POYNER

Millinery, Smart Coats and Gowns.
Tailored Costumes & Cardigan Suits.
Knitwear and Blouses.

☞ ALL AT MOST MODERATE PRICES.

**34 STATION ROAD, REDCAR.**   SPECIAL ATTENTION TO MOURNING ORDERS.

Redcar's ladies' fashion shop part-owner Sybil Wright (pictured), sister of Nancy Wright. Sybil had her own fashion shop in Station Road, with the very trendy name of 'Robina Brown'. It added that touch of ladies' clothing elegance to the road, if not the town.

Things were changing; this is the main entrance to the West Dyke Road shop, which is opposite the Clarendon Hotel. The window displays still look very dated.

The Nancy Wright Robina Brown fashion shop on West Dyke Road, after a refit in the late 1950s, by which time fashions were changing and the younger woman was demanding modern styles at more reasonable prices.

A cheerful Mrs Lowe hard at work making up orders and serving customers. Food rationing was still on when this photograph was taken as can be seen by the cards on the back wall which state 'your meat ration is 1s 2d'. What looks like a mincemeat machine can be seen on the far right.

George Lowe's family butcher's business dates back to the early days of market-stall trading, until establishing a family business in Redcar High Street. This photograph dates back to the late 1940s. On the left of Lowe's shop is Picknett's wet fish shop, and on the right with Austin car and petrol pumps, is Lambert's motor accessories, displayed in a house-type bay-windowed shop.

The very modern, open aspect of the central showroom of the Newhouse departmental store made for a greater variety of clothing to be displayed to its best advantage.

*Above:* The Marcel Wave hairstyle was becoming all the rage at the time of this Newhouse's fashion show – 'Fashions for all Occasions' – in the early 1930s. Here, staff members pose for a publicity shot by their in-house photographer. On the left is Rene Wright (*née* Stainsby).

*Right:* A late-1940s sales promotion of beach and swimwear by the staff of Newhouse Store. Standing is Joyce Thomas with colleague Kathleen Coan – the location is the flat roof of the store, suitably adorned with effective stage props!

Pictured here is Mr Marcus Coan, advertising manager of J. Newhouse Ltd. In addition to his artwork for advertisements in the local newspapers, Mr Coan also designed and made some mannequins used in window and fashion floor displays, which he skilfully constructed from laminated card covered with Plaster of Paris. Mr Coan retired in 1965 after a very inventive and fulfilling career.

Mrs Cissy Vallely, owner of the general dealers on the corner of Queen Street and Turner Street. Mrs Vallely and husband Mick allowed many locals to have groceries (except cigarettes) on tick. The many landladies in Turner Street were very thankful for this privilege over the years, because their visitors didn't pay them until the end of the week when they left.

Wilson's bread shop and bakery on Station Road, Redcar, in the 1930s, was well known for its good quality. The side entrance led to the large upstairs café. Some will remember, during the 1940s and '50s, queuing from six in the morning to be certain of the luxury of fresh bread and maybe some cream cakes!

Percy Pinkney's sweetshop, Garbutt Street, in Stockton, 1929. The family also had shops in Bernard Road, Bridge Road, and Piper's Bazaar, High Street. The Pinkneys were always considered respected confectioners and sugar boilers.

The photograph here shows Joe's Fish and Chip Saloon on West Dyke Road in Redcar. This photograph was taken in 1950 with the sun casting a shadow from the West: it is probably late afternoon or early evening. Notice the reflection in the shop windows of Sandringham and Buckingham Road opposite.

With a distinctive Art Deco design fish range as the backdrop, the staff of Joe's fish and chip saloon pose for a rare photograph in 1951. Left to right: Mary Snowdon, May Rigg, Emily Robinson, and Gertrude King. Joe's Fish and Chip Saloon was an extremely busy shop which often had a long queue down Holder Street.

# 4

# REDCAR FOR YOUR HOLIDAYS!

Teesside's popular weekend resort viewed from the pier. A large crowd around the Promenade slipway is watching Sunshine Corner – always a big attraction in pre-war days, but which never continued after the war.

Awaiting the arrival of HRH the Princess Royal for the christening of the RNLB *City of Leeds*, at the old Bandstand, Redcar, in August 1951. Crew members are, from left to right: Joey Hall, Harold Hall, Louis Playfoot, Ron Dixon, Jack Walton, Charles Cocks, Ron Williams and William Stonehouse.

An evening shot of the bandstand and central Promenade looking east. Note the illuminations around the Dome, indicating that it is late August or September; these were an added attraction to visitors at the end of the season.

Local fishermen did a fair trade in the summer season both before and after the war, taking day-trippers on pleasure trips: the cost was about two shillings. The gangway was a means of taking people to and from the boats without getting their feet wet! The Thompson, Picknetts, Kenyons, and others kept this business going up until the 1960s – with today's risk assessments and health and safety laws; it would be virtually impossible to operate now!

*Above:* A donkey ride is all part of a traditional holiday at the seaside. Rene Wright holds son Jim – the little girl on the right is thought to be a cousin. The small boy leading the donkey is probably working for the owners. Note the pier in the far distance – strange to see from this side, as the more lucrative trade for the donkey rides were always on the town side of the pier.

*Left:* A popular thing among the health-conscious ladies was to have your height and weight checked on your visit to Redcar. The two fashionably dressed ladies await the ticket from the man seated behind the scales, all for the price of one penny! Note the fashionable fox fur, which was quite acceptable then, but would be somewhat controversial today!

*Right:* In post-war years, on the same site as the previous photograph, Mrs Smith (left), with friend Mrs Robinson, carried on the tradition of checking your weight and height for some years on the Promenade at the top of the slipway, opposite Dundas Street.

*Below:* Prof. Will Fleet and his Punch and Judy show was a seaside institution and Redcar was no exception! The audience consists of mams and dads and the children are conspicuous by their absence!

*Above:* A glass of ice-cold milk on a hot summer's day was most refreshing – so was the message of the Government's 'drink more milk for health' campaign in the 1930s. The little boys on the right look to see if they have enough between them for a glass.

*Left:* Of further interest at the Dundas Slipway was this stainless steel drinking fountain of fresh cold water. By the amount of sand around the base of the fountain, it shows its other use of splashing water onto your sand-covered feet before putting your sandals back on.

When it was last warm enough to bathe in the sea at Redcar, Jack Wright captured the perfect holiday poster scene typical of the 1930s, complete with the fashionable bathing hats. From left to right are: Inga Wright, Daphne Wright, and friend.

The most popular part of Redcar beach was situated between the New Pavilion and the pier. This photograph was taken from the bandstand, showing clearly the Eldorado ice-cream stall. The kiosk with the domed roof sold fruit, sweets and daily newspapers.

Sandcastle and design competitions at Redcar and Saltburn in the late 1930s, organised by the *Daily Mail* and Cadbury's. A site was pegged out between the bandstand and the New Pavilion. Hundreds of children entered and all were guaranteed a prize of some sort. The event was very organised and orderly, with numbered pitches in neat rows.

This enormous piece of sand art, viewed from the pier, was created almost every day in the season, people would throw coins down onto a sheet laid out to reward the artist – seen crouching on the top left corner of picture.

*Above:* Billy Scarrow's 'Pierrots', who, by the 1937 coronation were known as the 'Optimists', performed throughout the summer in this large wooden building. It was also ideal to play on at extra high tides. Here, on centre stage, a little girl practises handstands, while the rest lark about.

*Right:* Prof. Foster, the ventriloquist, performed his show from the telephone-box sized hut at Redcar for many years, entertaining both children and parents. We all tried to see his lips move! Most of us referred to the show as 'the man with the talking doll', as we couldn't pronounce ventriloquist!

Ossy Kay's amusement arcade in the 1930s, known locally as 'The Dive', was a strange-looking building adjacent to the Coatham Hotel, with a mixture of architecture, part of which was pseudo-Tudor, part Baroque. The windows were painted over black. Oswald Kay died in the 1940s, and his wife Milly took over, later moving to Redcar High Street.

Pastimes Amusements, situated in the main Promenade between the Swan Hotel and Denney's Garage, was a very striking building in the Art-Deco style of the times. It was known as the White Elephant Arcade, but it did make money. Tommy Bestwick, the owner, later bought the next-door property, living upstairs. The ground floor was converted into a dodgem car track.

Free grandstand views of the Pierrot show from the Promenade. The very formally-dressed holiday crowd enjoy the comedy sketch, which varied from show to show throughout the week, with three shows daily plus a special midnight matinee, which was popular with landladies and late cinemagoers on warm August nights. It was a long day and little reward for the artistes, but it gave their landladies an opportunity to see their star guests actually perform.

Billy Scarrow and the 'Optimists' Pierrot show came to Redcar just after the First World War, and continued until 1939, the artists changing over the years. The then well-known comedian Billy Burden, later of television fame, was a member of the company for a number of years. Here we see a kiddie's talent competition in progress; the winners were decided by a show of hands.

Children's talent competition. There was no shortage of confident-looking youngsters for this show – perhaps Redcar's popular regular forerunner of *The X-Factor?*

Ann Goodman's Aunty Nance and Uncle Jack Taylor, with daughters Barbara and Penny, enjoying a week's holiday in 1947. They are seen here sitting on the beach between the New Pavilion shelters and bandstand. In the background can be seen Kiddies Corner, complete with a long '1p on the mat' slide.

The Coatham Enclosure. The boating lake, arguably the most ambitious project undertaken by Redcar Council in the 1930s, and funded by the government Development Aid Fund, which was targeted to help areas suffering from the industrial depression, contained two open-air swimming pools (one for adults, one for children), an indoor heated swimming pool, a boating lake, and a miniature golf course.

The ornamental bridge leading onto the island with shelter surrounded by flower gardens. Note the roof and surrounding enclosure festooned with illumination which transformed the whole boating lake into a fairyland of coloured lights at dusk in late August to September. Canadian-type canoes can be seen on the water, which were often capsized by over-enthusiastic young lads.

On busy bank holidays, the lake often got very congested. This photograph illustrates one such incident at the bridge, with three determined rowing boats having to make way for an aggressive-looking motor boat captain, in Trilby hat. Some find it amusing anyway!

Outdoor, cold seawater swimming pools on the north-east coast were not really a success unless it was a hot and sunny day. Two brave souls seem to be the only customers. It is, however, a splendid view of the Coatham Convalescent Home, now long gone and replaced by the leisure centre and car park.

A bright sunny day in 1936 attracts more swimmers seen here having a bit of fun trying to climb the rope ladder on the 'Bukta Ball'. Galas were held weekly – also water polo championships played during July and August. Of special interest were the sequence-swimming routines performed by the Eugene Mermaid Team of Young Ladies.

A contestant in the diving competition performs the swallow dive: local photographer Jack Wright catches the action. Note the tall Coatham Hotel building and houses of Newcomen Terrace that can be clearly seen.

The galas over, free time was then for all comers to have fun pushing the large float around the pool. Despite the council's efforts to attract swimmers, its popularity declined and the council began to lose money on this investment. People of course preferred the heated seawater indoor pool.

When the indoor heated seawater pool was officially opened in early 1931, it was an immediate success. A showpiece for it's time, one end of the pool was 3ft 6in deep and the adult end was 7ft 6in deep. In addition to this, it had an adjustable diving board and water slide. Hot and cold fresh water showers were also an added feature between the pool and changing cubicles. This early photograph shows a pool-side spectator seating area, which was later transferred to the upstairs balcony.

Redcar Amateur Swimming Club in the indoor baths in 1933. The club was the first to take advantage of the all-year-round use of the new facility – teaching learners to swim and experienced swimmers life-saving skills. Note that members all wore the standard, almost uniform-style, bathing costumes of the 1930s. George Ford is on the top step next to the white post.

At the outbreak of the Second World War in 1939 the outdoor pool was closed. It reopened in 1946, but was still poorly supported, except on warm sunny days when Joyce Thomas picked a perfect setting to pose for a bathing costume promotion on behalf of the Middlesbrough Newhouses department store in 1947. The little girls in the background are determined to get into the photograph!

*Above:* After the closure of the outdoor swimming pool in 1949, the council decided to convert the site into a roller-skating rink, which included a Poilite surface, at the overall cost of £10,000. This was a popular decision and the most cost-effective method as the underground changing rooms, and entrance buildings, were retained. The rink was officially opened by the town mayor, Councillor Cole, in 1951.

*Left:* Ann and Howard Goodman take a professional stance, council roller-skates could be hired for 6p but Ann preferred her own, with a gold-plated finish. Many enjoyable hours were spent with her brother and friend dancing to the popular music of the time, with of course occasional tumbles – witness the sticking plaster on Ann's knee.

*Right:* Going Dutch, Ann and Wendy Goodman having fun at one of the many carnival events at the rink in May 1951. The rink organised a hockey team made up of local boys, which did very well round the area.

*Below:* The miniature steam railway around the outer perimeter of the old outdoor swimming pool in 1948 was operated and driven by Gordon Trevitt, here seen with passengers Neville Pearson (second from the left) and Ernie Crust. Ian Denney can just be seen to the right of Ernie.

The giant racer, or 'figure of eight' as we called it, was a huge wooden lattice-work structure with a rail track which the small open carriages raced along. Other attractions were Noah's Ark, roller-skating and dodgem cars. The park was only two minutes from the town clock. It was opened in 1928 and closed in 1938. Land was sold to build Sandringham and Buckingham Roads.

An added attraction at the pleasure park was a visit from a one-legged stuntman known as Peg Leg Peggy who would dive from a 70ft-high tower into about 4ft of water. It is said that Peg Leg Peggy set himself ablaze before the dive. The holiday crowd gathered to watch as Peg Leg ascended the high tower for this death-defying leap.

With the crowd holding their breath, stuntman Peg Leg Peggy dives off the top board, silhouetted against the skyline: the captivated audience expect the worst.

A big splash as Peggy disappears into the tank, and all is well.

Many locals can clearly remember Sunshine Corner, with Uncle Tom and his concertina. He used to accompany a sing-along with words based around biblical stories. It is believed that Sunshine Corner was promoted by the Non-Conformist Church. The little children loved to sing along to such tunes as:

Sunshine Corner, oh it's jolly fine
It's for children under ninety-nine.
All are welcome, seats are given free
Redcar Sunshine Corner is the place for me!

A relaxed family audience on what appears to be a warm summer's day, encouraging support to friends singing in the competition, hoping to win a stick of Redcar Rock. Note Uncle Tom sitting on the steps to the stage! If the weather was wet or cold, Sunshine Corner was held in 'The Sunshine Hall', Station Road.

*Above:* A local group of The Women's League of Health and Beauty, giving a public demonstration to music at Redcar, 1937. The League was founded by Molly Stack in 1930, and was the forerunner to today's fitness obsession. The premature death of Molly from cancer in 1935 prompted Molly's daughter, Prunella, to take over the running of the League, which became world wide, with almost 100,000 members by 1937.

*Right:* Uniformly turned out with matching capes, the Women's League of Health and Beauty make their way off Redcar beach after the demonstration. The dark-haired lady accompanying the girls, next to the girl holding the white toy dog, may possibly be Prunella Stack.

An excellent view of the end of Redcar Pier, before its demise during the Second World War and from severe storm-damage over the years. The four boys larking about in the boat are probably junior members of the nearby Seagulls Swimming Club, which was a large wooden hut elevated on stilts above the normal high water line.

Redcar Pier was erected by Teesside firm of Head Wrightson. When completed, it was 300ft long from the esplanade, opposite Clarendon Street. The pier head featured a bandstand with shelters. There was also a small landing stage at the pier head for a paddle steamer that ran pleasure trips. This photograph, taken in 1936, shows the pier entrance, with shop and doorway to the large ballroom, built in 1907. The walking picture photographer was a regular visitor for the family season.

The right-hand side view of the pier entrance also showing the collection point shop for your snaps of walking pictures. To the right of this is the chocolate shop selling Rowntrees plain York chocolate. The people look to be a little overdressed to the modern eye, used to our casual dress standards. The lady on the left is wearing fox furs, which were very fashionable in the 1930s.

A seaside novelty photograph with your own face featured in one of these stage props was a real laugh to send home or to a friend at work.

Five-year-old Jim Wright with one of his dad's model boats at the paddling pool on the Stray, Redcar. These models were known as tok-tok powered boats. Small tin-plate versions like this one could be bought in the shops for a few pence.

Zetland Park at the East End of Redcar Promenade was unlike Locke Park at the West End of the town in that it had a more open aspect with bowling greens, tennis courts, and a crazy golf course. High fencing gave ample protection from the wind. Centre left can be seen a rose walk and an aviary.

This view of Zetland Park shows a small lake and on the right-hand side, tennis courts plus two grass courts.

Opened in the late 1920s, Locke Park is situated on the main road entrance to the town and covers 22 acres in extent. It boasts an ornamental boating lake, a large boathouse, six hard-court tennis courts, one bowling green, and a putting green. Boating was a very popular pastime on the tree-lined lake, with ample room for passing under the two bridges.

Swans soon established themselves on the islands round the lake. The trees have not yet developed as in the previous photograph! The structure of the giant racer and the Redcar gasworks gasometer can be clearly seen on the skyline.

A charabanc excursion to see the nearby area has just commenced its journey from the Promenade out towards Marske and along to Kirkleatham Gardens, for the visitors to look around the historic village and church, before finally making its way back to Redcar Promenade. The charabanc and horses were owned by Hartgrove Brothers, a well-known removal firm, and was driven by William Fleming.

# 5

# PEOPLE, ENTERTAINMENT & EVENTS

*Left:* The founding father of the Pacitto business was Giacomo Pacitto, who established his first ice-cream parlour in Norton Road, Stockton, later moving to Yarm Road. It wasn't until 1924 that the family opened their first ice-cream parlour on Redcar Promenade near the pier. It was known as the Nova Bar.

*Below:* Against strong competition, Pacitto's ice cream won a diploma and Gold medal from the ice-cream association in London in 1934 for its quality and perfection. It is now probably the only family business in Redcar making its own ice-cream on town premises.

Giacomo Pacitto's son, Alfredo, was later to take over the business, which by then had expanded to one shop on the High Street and another on the seafront (later to open the Stray café) and a window shop next to the New Pavilion.

Peggy Harris with her father Alf Harris on her wedding day in 1936. Peggy was referred to locally as the most beautiful woman in Redcar! She married Alfredo Pacitto at the Sacred Heart Church in Redcar, later becoming manageress in the Redcar shops.

*Above:* This line-up of lovely ladies from 1936 are members of the Seagulls Amateur Swimming Club – Clarice Playfoot (*née* Ford), is second from right. Note the end of the pier in the background and the little boy with his back to the camera – what is he doing with his back to the camera? Your guess is as good as mine!

*Left:* This photograph shows a dejected-looking horse and barefooted rider waiting for customers to hire the bathing machine. You got into the machine and changed within it whilst still on the beach, the machine was then pulled out into the sea, and after your swim, you returned to the machine, changed, and were then brought back and descended onto the dry beach. Their use declined, and by 1921 the council had twenty-four bathing tents, each a little larger than a telephone box, setting them on the beach for a daily rental of 6*d*.

Lifeboat Day in the 1930s was as popular then as it is today. Seen in all its splendour is the *Louisa Polden*, Redcar's first motor boat. Redcar has a long association with the lifeboat service and is proud of its record of lives saved.

Always a popular attraction with the day-trippers was the spectacle of the lifeboat launching. A special launching trailer with a 'case' caterpillar tractor was constructed for the important work. The *Louisa Polden* gave outstanding service from 1931-1951, saving many lives in the seas around Redcar's treacherous coastline.

A crowd gather at the beach, possibly around a swimmer who got into difficulties. Seabathing could be hazardous, as we see in this photograph taken from the east side of the pier railings. Incidents like this were quite regular, with strong undercurrents carrying inexperienced swimmers out of their depth. It is quite possible one of the trained life savers from the Swimming Club on the right has recovered the unfortunate swimmer.

Louis Playfoot (right) is working on the outboard motor which he used for his speedboat in the late 1930s. One of his staff, Colin Coates (left), is operating the lathe in the Turner Street garage at Coatham, Redcar. Louis was a well-liked man who always had a laugh and joke. In the late 1950s Louis opened a new Vauxhall agency on the High Street. Note the long, exposed overhead belt drives, not allowed today, but quite common practice years ago. Louis Playfoot also had an interest in speedboats and built a small hydroplane, to which he fitted a powerful racing Elto outboard motor. Louis had no particular name for his boat so he named it *Itsa* for want of a better name!

*Above and below:* On the evening of 16 August 1939, Louis Playfoot and Laurie Denney were both enjoying the rare opportunity of some high-speed boat fun on a flat calm sea just off Redcar beach. Laurie was near Redcar Pier. Louis was up the Coatham end when suddenly Louis' engine burst into flames. Laurie, on seeing the glow in the skyline over Hartlepool, thought it was a brilliant sunset – which was normal at the time of year. Realising that it must be Louis's boat on fire, he raced at full speed to the rescue.

Joe Heathcock was a voluntary auxiliary fireman in Redcar during the Second World War. He was on call twenty-four hours a day, seven days a week, as well as being a fish-fryer and running his own fish and chip shop business in West Dyke Road. Fish and chips were one of the few items of food not on ration during the conflict.

Police Sergeant Buckton, pictured here outside his home in Sycamore Road in Redcar, on the day of his retirement. Sergeant Buckton had served in the police at Castleton, Lingdale, Loftus, Dormanstown, and finally Redcar, in 1942. He was station sergeant at Redcar and in charge of inquiries into the accidental shooting by a member of Redcar home guard and a regular army soldier stationed at Marske.

Laurie Denney started in the garage business in 1928 with his shop on the High Street, and the garage round the corner in Moore Street, before moving to its present Promenade site. Standing is Ken Marshall, with boss Laurie Denney seated, having a bit of fun in a customer's Austin Seven sports racing car in Moore Street, *c.* 1930.

Laurie Denney always had a liking for American cars and owners would receive his personal attention – here Laurie prepares to take this Chrysler for a road test.

Middlesbrough Motor Club's annual speed trials at Saltburn were held in July and attracted up to 60,000 people to the town for the car and motorcycle races. Additional bus and train services were needed, to cater for the masses arriving. It was held on the stretch of sands between Saltburn and Marske. Here, Winterschladen's lorry (caterers for the event) acts as a club-member grandstand for a better view of the races in 1936.

Car and motorcycle speed trials, first staged at Saltburn and in later years on Coatham Sands, Redcar, were organised by the Middlesbrough Motor Club and attracted thousands of people to Redcar. Here we see 'Gilly' Bensley from Middlesbrough at his best on his racing Norton in 1938, winning the 350cc race. Tragically, Gilly lost his life while serving in the RAF in the Second World War in operations over Germany.

Harry Hartgrove with Horace Barker (seated), after winning an award at the Stokesley Agricultural Show in the late 1950s.

August 1937. The scene of the Cleveland Agricultural Show on Redcar racecourse, with the dog show in progress. In the background is the old grandstand and Tote, quite easily recognised. The marquee on the left would be one of several to display a variety of farming stock as well as a home-grown produce stall, handicrafts and hobbies, such as photography.

No longer seen today, the all-animal circus was a regular visitor to Redcar, in the 1930s. It was usually on a site known as Beans Field at the bottom of West Dyke Road, which terminated just after Brooksbank Avenue. A controversial subject now, but the circus was extremely popular years ago.

High seas on the slipway encouraged children to play the game of 'wave chasing', which here creates great excitement. It appears harmless, but in extreme sea conditions is highly dangerous, and most unwise.

An interested audience look on as a stall-holder demonstrates his special way of making omelettes on market day, Wednesday 4 September 1944. This is thought to be Stockton, but he would have plied his trade in all markets in the area. In those hard days of wartime rationing, an omelette would be made with dried egg. Note the paraffin Primus stove – no risk assessment then!

Redcar's traditional Wednesday market has long been at the top end of the High Street, but was by no means the only one. However in the 1930s it attracted huge crowds, the large variety of stalls extended from the far end of the High Street to the Redcar Lane end. This stall, selling crockery, was a regular for many years.

A novel and inventive way of constructing a coronation coach using a juvenile's three-wheeled bike. A considerable amount of time and effort must have been spent in the organising of the parade. The little girl pedals furiously to keep up, while dad keeps an eye on her progress – seen here heading for Albert Park, Middlesbrough, in May 1937.

The ever-popular marching band leads the coronation fancy dress from Linthorpe Road into Albert Park. The crowds of spectators blocking the road hold up the double-decker bus in front of what was then McAdam's Garage.

The smiles on the faces of the large crowd show amusement at the very life-like Gandhi, and the lady flower seller. In the background one can clearly see the Dorman Museum.

Large crowds gather outside the Dorman Museum to applaud local contestants as they make their way for judging. The boy drummers lead, then a Stone-Age man, an Indian warrior, and the Devil.

*Left:* Judging over, class winners pose for Jack Wright's camera. On the left is Drag Artist (2nd prize), followed by a Means Test protester, making a political point by holding half a loaf of bread which would probably be used later in a bread pudding!

*Below:* All the Newport-area street kids strain to get in the photograph on this memorable occasion in 1937. Now the games can begin!

Thornaby aerodrome hosted Empire Air Days in 1934, 1935 and 1937, attracting large numbers of Thornaby and Teesside residents. The aerodrome was close to the town and local bus stops. This massive hangar was used for exhibits and displays on Empire Day, and evidently a tea stall as well!

Thornaby Empire Air Day was an opportunity for many ordinary people to see a low-flying aircraft and close up on the ground for the first time. This aircraft is an Avro Anson and one of 233 Squadron, which moved to Thornaby in 1937. It became a common sight over Teesside in the years following.

Handley Page Hereford bomber outside No. 1 hangar (which burned down during the national firemen's strike in 1978). It's unbelievable that this antiquated bi-plane was still in service in the late 1930s. Note the open cockpit and wooden propellers.

This Hawker Demon was part of the North Riding 608 Squadron Auxiliary Air Force, Thornaby. It would be a schoolboy's dream to get this close to a real aircraft. The bungalows in the far distance are on Millbank Lane; this photograph was taken where Martinet Road is today.

For a number of summers in the 1930s, flying displays and pleasure flights were given at Redcar by Sir Alan Cobham's Flying Circus, officially known as the National Aviation Display Ltd. These visits were always well attended. The field at the end of the Coast Road between Redcar and Marske was the site used, which is now the playing field of Byedales School. Parachutist Harry Ward is seen climbing into the cockpit of the Tiger Moth.

This Handley-Page W10 eight-seater passenger plane at Marske, awaits customers, on a chilly August evening in 1934. The aircraft crashed in Buckinghamshire on 22 September of the same year!

On the whole the displays were safe, and there was no shortage of paying customers. The normal cost for a flight was 10s, which was to take part in the opening formation flight in the programme, or for 5s, a short four-minute joy ride. On a good day twelve such flights could be slotted into a one-hour period.

Observer Corps volunteers. Throughout the war, Queen Street shop owner Mick Vallely (left) with a colleague, was on duty at the Coatham links post. The piece of technical equipment is for plotting the direction, approach, and height of enemy aircraft.

Redcar ATC/300 Squadron based at Coatham Grammar School. In less than a year the squadron had 150 members. This group of schoolboys line up in front of the Memorial Hall – the hall is still in use today, but the grammar school has long gone, replaced by the council libraries building. Back row, from left to right: Bill Pashley, Steve Backer, Jack Cox, Maurice Piggot, -?-, Edgar Robinson, Keith Barraclough, ? Hamer. Middle row: W/O Freddie Watson, Cpl Charles Robinson, -?-, -?-, -?-, Les Wilson, Bob Carter, ? Spence, Keith Burns, George Bealse, Cpl Geoff Tate. Front row: -?-, ? Carter, ? Close, -?-, ? Powell, -?-, -?-, Donald Dodsworth, -?-.

Coatham Grammar School playground was chosen for this photograph, taken in 1942, of would-be aircraft engineer mechanics receiving instruction from experienced aircraft builder Laurie Denney (standing next to aircraft engine). The uniformed officer on the right is flying officer Cox, and standing next to him is Ken Marshall in white overalls. The uniformed officer with hands clasped in front is pilot officer Frank Colley. Other boys in the crowd are Billy Chilmade, Bill Chance, Richard Morris, and Bob Warrior.

A military band stirs the patriotism within these young boys – the annual camp at Marske of the Green Howards Territorials on this occasion is seen marching along the Redcar-Marske Coast Road, just passing Well's Grove Junction. The new houses in the background had recently been built, the one on the left is still for sale!

Back to normal and let's go to Redcar races! Thousands of racegoers stream out from the West Dyke Road course on August Bank Holiday Monday 1949, heading back to the railway and bus station. In the foreground on the right is Clubley's tobacconist's kiosk, also top right is the roof of West Dyke School.

*Right:* The sheer volume of racegoers almost becoming a logjam for the five cars at the West Dyke Road railway crossing. Note the old wooden railway bridge, a favourite of the West Dyke schoolchildren if it could be timed so they could be on top and a steam train passed beneath.

*Below:* A slight bump with the old town bus service United on the Redcar to Marske Coast Road in the mid-1930s. The bus driver inspects the damage with the local bobby close behind. The bus conductress stands back from it all. Note the policeman wears puttees. The small hut in the background is a council putting green office.

February 1953 will go down in history along the east coast of England as bringing one of the worst storms ever experienced! The gales in early February left a trail of unprecedented havoc at Redcar and Saltburn – although other local seaside resorts badly damaged were Staithes, Sandsend, and Robin Hood's Bay, and others all down the east coast. Redcar Pier ballroom was closed for the Saturday Night Dancing because of high seas lashing underneath the structure, causing the ballroom floor to be damp.

The GPO telephone box has collapsed into the cavity beneath the pavement along a large section of sea wall, as can be seen by the man inspecting the damage – the strong wind was still blowing.

With the tide out and a lull in the storm, looking up from the beach, the damage to the sea wall and steps can be fully appreciated. The white Nova Bar on the far left was the very popular Pacitto's ice-cream parlour.

Looking west down from the pier ballroom entrance, the extent of damage to the sea wall is more appreciated. The fishing boats were luckily undamaged.

A view from the east side of the pier. The steps and iron railings, broken and twisted, was a scene of devastation. The Seagull Swimming Club's headquarters and a tea hut were also washed out to sea!

Standing back to see how the sea wall foundations had been washed away, the house-owners on the Promenade must have been terrified at the height of the storm. Note the well-known Rea's ice-cream parlour on the left of the photograph.

Most of the damage caused by the high seas and gale-force winds was concentrated around the pier area, however two sections of the Promenade in front of the Stray were badly damaged. At the bandstand end of the Promenade, the sea burst open the doors of the first-aid room and deckchair storerooms and washed away a stack of deckchairs.

The slipway has collapsed and railings snapped, with the Royal Hotel sustaining only slight external damage.

Our attention now moves out of Redcar along the coast to Saltburn, where we see families on an organised church or social club annual trip to the seaside for the children, funded by small all-the-year-round saving schemes. Here we see a crowd of parents and children taking part in some organised sports, just near the Skelton Beck outlet in 1936.

Saltburn's Bankside café in the late 1930s. Saltburn in the pre-war days was considered to be a more sedate town than Redcar, with no amusement arcades or loud music. Emphasis was more on the Valley Gardens (the 'Italian Gardens'), woodland walks, the pier, and miles of beautiful coastal views from the Promenade, most immediately noticeable of which were the nearby cliffs.

Sand design competitions organised by Cadbury's were a popular part of the seaside holiday scene in the 1930s. These well-organised children's competitions were normally oversubscribed, with several hundred entries. Each child was allotted a small, numbered plot to work in. The standard of artwork was high, and no child went home without a big bar of Cadbury's chocolate. This event, on a warm summer day, was at Saltburn in 1937. The site is on the west side of the pier. Note the Bankside buildings.

In 1936, at the side of the cliff lift, we have a clear view of Bankside café and bungalow. Apart from some changes the café, which has been turned into a pub, and the land on the right (now a car park), little has changed.

```
TO-NIGHT ! !
           THE
LITTLE    THEATRE,
THE  PIER .................... SALTBURN-BY-THE-SEA.

Opening Performance of
       the Season.

The Little Theatre
    CABARET.
(Under the direction of HARRY TOLLFREE.)

ALICE SOUTHCOTE, Soprano.
    JACKSON BROWNE, Comedian.
        CONSTANCE HOGBEN, Solo Pianist.
            EDWARD SYDNEY, Entertainer.
                DORIS COLLETT, Comedienne.
                    HARRY TOLLFREE, Baritone.

EVERY EVENING AT 8 p.m.
2/-  (Basket   1/6   1/-  (Including
     Chairs).               Tax).

Booking Office :—Saltburn Cafe, Ltd. Tel. Saltburn 103.
    All Seats Bookable.    No extra charge.
                Page 9.
```

*Above:* The famous Saltburn landmark of Huntcliff and Cat Nab in the late 1930s. The beach huts bordering the shoreline have long gone. The old wooden café has now been replaced, and a car park today takes the area where the caravan stands in the picture.

*Left:* In 1935, for the princely sum of *2s*, one got the luxury of the night's entertainment in Saltburn Pier Theatre in one of the best basket chairs.

*Above:* A strange and intriguing photograph from Saltburn, this one from the late 1920s. The two ladies with Japanese paper parasols seem confident in patting the calf, while the calf's mother in the background seems unconcerned. The damaged pier in the background is undergoing repair.

*Right:* Saltburn Pier in the 1930s. The Little Theatre here presented cabaret performances every evening in the summer season, under the direction of Harry Tollfree.

Saltburn's Mr Bert Grapho's pierrots in 1937, known as the 'Jovial Jollies'. The stage was on the lower Promenade at the top of the slipway on the west side of the pier. The troop had forty years association with Saltburn. This day in August when the photograph was taken appears to have been not well attended: the 'Jovial Jollies' are singing their socks off with the audience conspicuous by their absence!

Saltburn's Promenade photographer takes a snap of Rene Wright on the lower Promenade, as her husband Jack takes a picture for the family album in 1937.

The Stead Memorial Hospital annual fund-raising ball held in the pier ballroom, Redcar, in 1930. The hospital was bequeathed to the town by the Dr J.E. Stead, a distinguished metallurgist, on the understanding that funds would have to be raised by the town to maintain it. The mayor (John Emerson Batty) and mayoress (both centre front row) are accompanied by local councillors and members of the medical profession. Note the lifebelts and ship's bell giving a nautical flavour.

Danny Mitchell and his orchestra were resident at the pier ballroom, Redcar, from 1949 onward. His orchestra was exceptionally versatile in that Danny would present it as the 'Hawaiians' one-day with Brenda Oliver as an Hawaiian dancer and vocalist, and the next day a small sextet suitable for cabaret with Brenda playing in the band. Afternoon tea dances called Café Continental were also popular on wet afternoons.

In pre-war days the Swan Hotel was another popular dance hall. A number of different bands would play there throughout the year. It is claimed to have had the best sprung dance floor in town.

Ken Marshall and his band played in the Swan Hotel for many years. The band was largely made up of Redcar musicians. Second from left is Charlie Skinner on saxophone, second from right at the front is Sidney Strickland on trumpet. The lady vocalist is Fay, with Ken Marshall on bass standing next to her.

*Above:* Charles Amer and his orchestra. Back row, from left to right: Stan Able, trumpet; Peter Beer, trumpet; Gene Jarred; Ron Melber, trombone. Front row: bandleader Bob Dalcin (standing), saxophone; Ken Francis, saxophone; Ron Hunt, saxophone; Johnny Marshall, saxophone; Ron Hutchinson, baritone saxophone. Top left is Max Clark on drums, also in the band but just out of picture, Norman Drummond on piano and Howard Kershaw on bass.

*Right:* Drummer in the Charles Amer band, Max Clarke, indulges in one of his party tricks – cameraman Derek Richardson catches the drumstick in mid-air to backup Max's talents!

# CHARLES AMER & HIS FAMOUS ORCHESTRA

PLAY FOR DANCING EVERY
WEDNESDAY & SATURDAY
AT THE

### COATHAM HOTEL REDCAR

15 star musicians
With featured B.B.C. Vocalist

### Carole Scott

Under the personal supervision of the Smiling Maestro of the Screen,

### CHARLES AMER

WATCH THIS COLUMN FOR NEW FEATURES WEEKLY WITH GUEST ARTISTES AND EVENTS OF INTEREST.

Tel. 83.     Tel. 83.

*A rather flattering publicity photograph of myself, resplendent in full evening attire taken around 1947.*

---

### TEES-SIDE...
# PRESS BALL
**COATHAM HOTEL REDCAR**

NOVEMBER 6th, 1958

with

CHARLES AMER and ORCHESTRA

☆ ☆ ☆ ☆

**by Peter the Panda**

As I'm the mascot for this Press Ball, they've let me have the job of giving a big welcome to everyone who's come along tonight.

I'm the first mascot they've ever had, and they say if everyone doesn't have a good time the blame will be put on ME. I'm supposed to bring them luck!

So for the sake of keeping me out of trouble, PLEASE enjoy yourselves, will you?

Seriously, though, thank you all for turning up. Our aim is to give you lots of fun, but the money you spend will help to make life brighter for many needy people.

After each Press Ball the profits are given to two worthy charities, and we hope the cheques posted off this year will be as big as ever.

Now, on with the Ball!! I'll be watching how things go from my place among the prizes. Then I'll be off home with one of you in the early hours.

Yes, even their own lucky mascot is going as a prize. Well, some little boy or girl will be pleased to see me in the morning!

---

*Above:* Arguably the most popular dancehall in Redcar in the post-war years was the Coatham Hotel, when the well-known hotel owner Charles Amer and his orchestra was in residence.

*Left:* Many private functions were staged in the Coatham Hotel. One was the annual Press Ball for Teesside. The money raised at this dance went to local charities.

Dennis Beales' band playing in the Queen's Hotel, Redcar, in the late 1950s. From left to right: Geoff Cox, trumpet; Jim Wright, guitar; Dennis Beales, drums; Syd Mould, clarinet; Les Giles, accordion and Joe Bolton, piano. Dennis was the first to play at the Park Hotel on its opening in the late 1950s and also started a jazz club there.

Private functions were a speciality with Dennis Beales. His newly-formed 'Four in Accord' band, seen here playing at Scorby Manor Jazz Club, Scarborough in 1957, proudly presenting his new band jackets and music stands. Dennis was also backing for Ronnie Scott and Karl Baritone at the club. From left to right: Dennis Beales, drums; Lou Robinson, saxophone; Joy Bannister, bass and Roy Bannister, piano.

The Phil Raine jazz band was originally formed by a group of Redcar musicians whose main interest was Dixieland jazz. The founder musicians in the 1950s were Phil Raine on trumpet, Gerry Bickerstaffe on clarinet, Jim Wright on guitar, Pete Jackson on piano, Des Snaith on drums, and Dave Keen on trombone.

A variety of venues were played, from Teesside to as far afield as Scarborough. The band didn't stay together in this form for long, as players seen playing several years later are Phil Raine on trumpet, Johnny Crisp from Billingham on trombone, Jim Wright on guitar and George Nelson from Hartlepool, on piano.

One of the many annual private club dinner dances at the Coatham Hotel – this one is possibly the Redcar Rugby Club dance in 1958. From left to right, back row: Jack Wright, Bill Elliott, Brian Peacock, Ian Denney, Val Leighton, Jim Wright, Kay Tunstall, Rene Wright. Front row: Mike Gray and Brian Pinkney. The photograph was taken by well-known Redcar photographer, Derek Richardson.

An all-ladies band in a delightfully decorated far-eastern setting, in 1936. The venue is unknown – it may be a cinema café in one of the many cinemas on Teesside.

The very 1930s-style New Pavilion, with Pacitto's windows sales shop on the left. The shop on the right is a rickshaw hire service! The Pavilion even had its own commissionaire!

In 1946, Barry Wood opened his seaside summer show at the New Pavilion, Redcar entitled Radio Tymes. The shows were very popular and were made up of a talented and versatile cast of good family entertainers – Barry is on the far right.

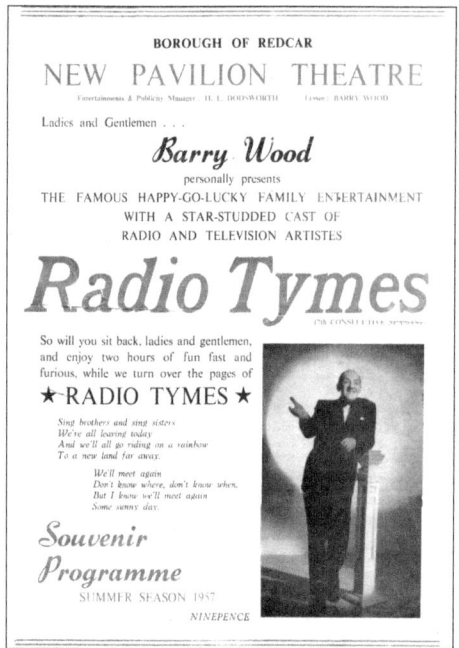

*Above left:* The shows continued for years. The cover here is from ten years on, with the Radio Tymes show becoming almost an institution in the area.

*Above right:* In the 1950s, Larry Grayson was the star comedian and a female impersonator in the Radio Tymes. Larry's stage name was Billy Breen, and his catchphrase, 'shut that door', made him a favourite of the Teesside audiences and well remembered long after Larry became host of the BBC's *Generation Game*.

In the 1930s, in pre- and post-seasons, the New Pavilion hired out their theatre for Sunday performances of light orchestral music, to accommodate the demand for entertainment on the Sabbath without offending the Sabbath Day observance standards, as it was a respectable alternative to boisterous variety shows.

The Regent Cinema, Redcar, was occasionally hired by the Redcar and District Amateur Operatic Society for their productions. This production is presumably from 1937 and thought be the *Quaker Girl* or maybe the *Country Girl*, if the latter, then it was staged at the New Pavilion on 1 December 1947.

*Left:* Audrey Jowsey from Redcar on stage in a Middlesbrough Little Theatre production of *1066 And All That* at St John's Hall, Middlesbrough. Audrey played three parts – sunbather, sailor, and French girl. Here we see Audrey in the 'Canute' scene from the show. This ran from 25 March to 6 April 1946.

*Below:* The Redcar Amateur Operatic Society musical comedy romance *Carissima* staged at the Pavilion in 1953. Dancers in the production were, from left to right: Aileen Livingstone, Pat Moor, Ellen Brolly, Janet Beadle, Ann Clemmit, and Lily Ward. The production and choreography were by Maisy Griffiths.

*Opposite above:* Alan Gale, a Redcar man, was a talented performer and later a producer of pantomime at the Theatre Royal, Middlesbrough in the early 1950s. People on Teesside will remember Alan Gale's Pierrots on the beach with his troupe 'The Wavelets', who performed in the summer season consecutively from the years 1946 until 1950. Later, Alan became interested in old-time music hall, returning to Redcar, to the delight of his many loyal friends, when he produced this old-time music hall show, in the Pavilion (now the Regent cinema). At least the show would not be at the mercy of the weather as his al fresco Pierrot 'Alan Gales Wavelets' outdoor shows were in the early post-war years.

*Another Diary Date*

## New Pavilion Theatre, Redcar

The Society have pleasure in announcing that they have engaged the services of . . .

### ALAN GALE

who will present a full professional company in

ALAN GALE
A Redcartonian now well up the Show-Biz ladder — One of the most sought after Producers in the country today.

## The Gay Nineties

An Olde Tyme Music Hall Entertainment direct from six successful seasons at Margate.

**SATURDAY, JUNE 30th, to SATURDAY, AUGUST 25th**

Change of programme weekly

Prices of Admission: 4/-, 3/-, 2/6

Evenings at 7-45 p.m.
Saturdays at 6 and 8-15 p.m.

PATRICIA KAY
One of the stars of THE GAY NINETIES. Gifted with a lovely voice she also has the assets of acting ability combined with great personal charm.

## THE "BACK ROOM" BOYS ... AND GIRLS

Stage Manager : Derek S. Copeland
Asst. Stage Managers : Wilf. Graham and Peter Sellman
"Props" : Betty Pickering and Hilda Copeland
Wardrobe Master : Jack Turnbull
Wardrobe Mistress : Vi Nicholson assisted by May Chamberlain
"Electrics" : Len Lozman
Stage Carpenter : Frank Stangroom
Prompt : Joan Bottomley
Call-"boy" : Anne Pickering
Make-up by : Stan Ross and Edith Sinclair
Hon. Stage "Hands" :
C. Graham, Harry Moss, Ian Moutrey, David Price
Hon. First Aid Attendant : Herbert Stainthorpe, B.R.C.S.

### OUR PRODUCER

Verne Morgan, one of the National Operatic & Dramatic Association's top producers, will be remembered for his first-rate production of our last show — "NO, NO NANETTE." He has endeared himself to the Society so much that he has already been booked to produce future shows for us including the pantomime in January, 1963.

He has recently completed the production of "FLOWER DRUM SONG" for North Staffs. Amateur Operatic Society — one of the first Society's to present this latest show by Rogers & Hammerstein.

**VERNE MORGAN**

Below: *Peter Pan* was the pantomime production by Marjorie Lucas and Dorothy Foster, who were the main people behind the Parish Players. The orchestra was composed of local musicians. Note that Frank Kyle was the violinist – a teacher at James McKinley School, Redcar, at the time.

### NEW PAVILION, REDCAR.

## PETER PAN

AT 7 P.M. PROMPT

### NEW YEAR'S DAY

AND

### SATURDAY, JAN. 6th, 1945

Produced by :
DOROTHY FOSTER & MARJORIE LUCAS.

ORCHESTRA :
Pianist Conductor .......... Dorothy Foster
Leader ........................ Mrs. Lowther
Violins ....................... Mr. Frank Kyle
                              Mr. Frank Wigham
Cello ......................... Mr. Sid Waddleton
Flute ......................... Mr. Scott
Clarionet ..................... Mr. A. Waller
Saxaphone .................... Mr. Harry Teesdale
Trumpet ....................... Mr. Jim Taylor
Drums ......................... Mr. Roy Birch

Stage Manager ................ Mr. Norman Watts

Script and Ensemble by Marjorie Lucas.
Musical Director ... Dorothy Foster.

Under the auspices of
REDCAR PARISH CHURCH
Proceeds in aid of Redcar Church Institute Appeal Fund.

PRICE - THREEPENCE.

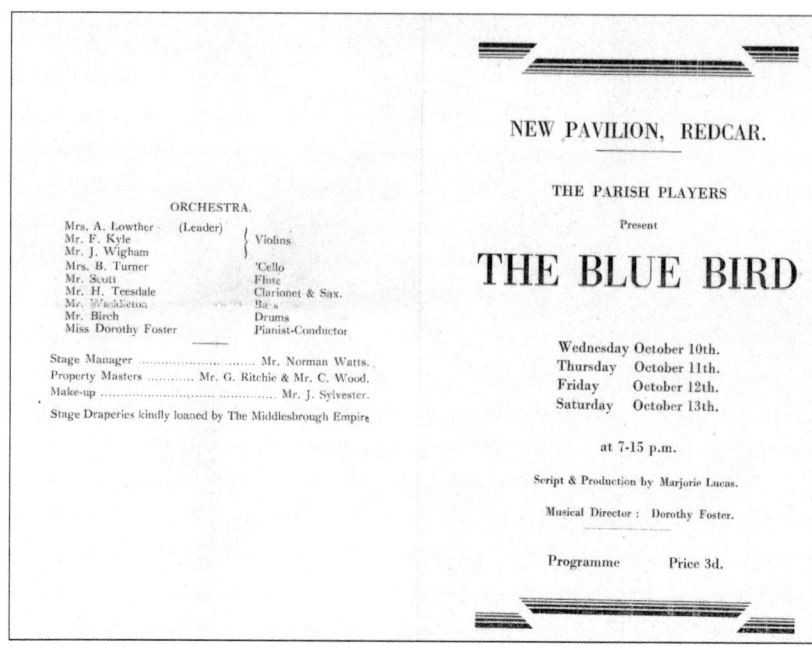

Programme for the 'Redcar parish church plays' presentation of *The Blue Bird*, when Redcar girls, Noreen Blackburn and Barbara Jowsey first experienced the thrill of 'treading the boards' in front of a live audience.

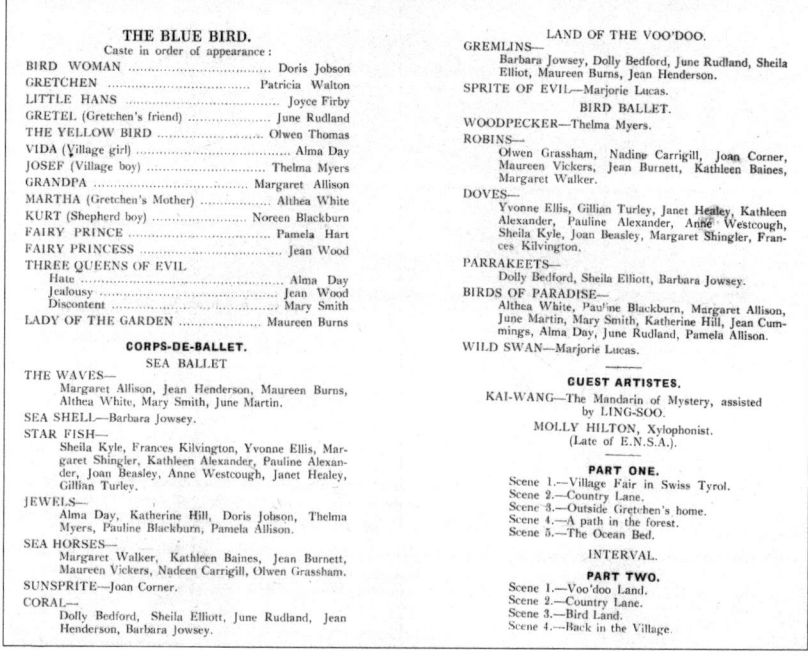

The cast list of players in *The Blue Bird* in 1946. Some of the multi-talented girls were playing more than one role.

# 6

# SCHOOLS & SPORTS

John Emerson Batty School, situated at the east end of Redcar, was built in 1929, but officially opened in 1930 by the then current Redcar Mayor, after whom the school was named. This infant class of six- or seven-year-olds look happy learning the building blocks of life. The teacher here is possibly a Miss Nicholson.

Looking out from the John Emerson Batty School onto Laburnum Road at the east end of Redcar – the school was designed and built along the lines of the new age; a very light and airy design, incorporating many glass panels and a glass canopy, which was found to be both too hot in the summer, and extremely cold in the winter.

Saltburn High School girls outside the school extension on Mill Lane in 1947. From left to right, back row: Marjorie Wilson, Barbara Sutton, Audrey Linton, Jean Beaton, Marjorie Bothroyd, June Branton. Middle row: Lorna Hudson, Joan Watson, Jean Harrison, Doreen Winter, Dorothy Ward, Maureen Metcalfe, Lena Knaggs. Front row: Elsie Craggs, Patricia Gill, Maureen Rutherford, Mary Harwood, Leila Williams.

The class of Mrs Florence Sill's Shorthand and Typing School. Teaching was conducted in her large house on Nelson Terrace, Redcar. A typical course for becoming fully qualified for employment as a secretary would last between nine and twelve months. This happy class of Redcar girls was taken in the late 1940s. Maureen Rutherford is second from right at the front; Margaret Ward is third from the right in the back row.

Red House School Saltburn junior cricket team in the late 1950s. From left to right, back row: Dicker, Brown, Carnegie, Waiton, Kershaw, Renshaw, Wilkinson. Middle row: Harwood, McCallum, Leyfield, McDonald, Allison. Front row: Pacitto, McKay, Askew, Rudd.

John Emerson Batty School junior football team 1937/8 photograph taken in the garden of No. 73 Borough, Road Redcar. From left to right back row: Willis, Burnett, Goldsborough, Hyde, Short, Berry. Middle row: Ramshaw, Meadours, Robson (Captain), Parker, Gittins. Front Row: Hibbert, Corel, Fowler.

Cleveland Youth Organisation Football League Championship winners, Redcar – the photograph shows the boys at Borough Park about 1945. Also winners of the youth club championship (large cup). From left to right, back row: Vincent Low, Bob Hewgill, Arnie Shinner, -?-, Brian Airy, Allen Saddler, Wilf Hammond, -?-, and club leader Jimmy Hill. Front row: Ged Cohen, Bernard Milner, Gordon Fowler, Des Boak, Colin Hill, Ken Kirby.

Coatham Grammar School, Redcar, rugby team XV of winter 1942/3 and 1944. From left to right, back row: 'Leach, McDonald, Hudson, Hetherington, Bell, -?-, Lauriston. Middle row: Wedgwood, Shawcross, -?-, -?-, -?-, Reid. Front Row: Hunt (later to become governor of the Faulklands Islands during the conflict), -?-, Underwood.

This happy bunch of Sunday school children were enjoying a special coronation trip out to the seaside at Saltburn in 1937. The pamphlet held proudly for the camera is a souvenir of the coronation of King George VI and Queen Elizabeth.

VE Day celebrations in May 1945 at Sandringham Road, Redcar. Laurie Picknett is centre-right of the picture dressed as a woman. At the end of the war VE Day and VJ Day street parties were held all over the country.

# 7
# REDCAR AT WAR

The Home Guard in action on the Eston Hills firing range.

*Redcar's Tragic War Accidents*
A sergeant and approximately eight men of the 4th Battalion Green Howards Home Guard, Redcar, stationed in a Nissen Hut on the Stray opposite Zetland Park, patrolled in pairs for a two-hour stint, from dusk to dawn.

On the night in question two privates of the platoon set off along their section of the sea front up to the designated boundary with Marske, unknown to them both, a regular army soldier from Marske Camp was patrolling from the opposite direction.

The strict blackout in force made it difficult to see anything. The patrol sentry, who had been a First World War soldier, challenged a figure coming out of the gloom 'Halt, who goes there?' – no reply. Three challenges – 'Halt, who goes there?' – no reply. When there was no reply after three challenges the sentry did fire, killing the soldier from Marske Camp.

There was a big enquiry, which caused quite a stir at the time; the outcome was that the private was completely exonerated. One can only imagine how the private felt afterwards – he was in a terrible emotional state, and a broken man. These incidents did happen in wartime, but for the sentry – he was never the same again.

An inquest was held and the widow of the soldier who was shot travelled from the south of England to identify the body. Police Sergeant Buckton of the North Riding Constabulary was involved in the enquiry and described the incident to the widow. It transpired that she had been unhappy in the marriage. Her husband had been a violent man and had also been unfaithful. On learning this, Sergeant Buckton arranged for her to see the unfortunate sentry in private to relate her story. In short, she said she was glad to be rid of him. Obviously the sentry was relieved to some extent, but he never got over the unfortunate incident.

These tragic fatalities throughout the war years were not confined to service personnel. They were at least four other deaths to civilians. Two young Warrenby boys lost their lives going through the barbed wire and into the minefield on Coatham Golf Links, while searching in the long Marrana Grass. Local golfers would pay half a crown – the equivalent of about £5 at today's prices, for a hard-to-get Dunlop golf ball. As one can imagine, this was a huge incentive for young boys, who would not in those days be getting any pocketmoney, to risk venturing through the wire, with the consequent tragic results.

On 4 June 1942, a little London evacuee girl, aged six, who was staying with her auntie in Hawthorn Road, wandered off with a friend aged four, crossing the Redcar to Marske Coast Road onto the Stray. The girl found a small gap in the barbed wire and crawled into the minefield, with the little boy following. The little girl stepped onto a mine and was killed – the little boy was seriously injured.

Although the Second World War did not start until 3 September 1939, it had been imminent since the Munich crisis in 1938. The country was put on a war footing. With the withdrawal of the British Expeditionary Force from France in June 1940, at home, gas masks were issued. Almost overnight, the military moved in, and Redcar became a garrisoned town. Two sections of the pier were removed and the Promenade access roads were restricted, with huge concrete barricades, with just enough room for one person to pass through. Several of the larger seafront houses were commandeered by the military authorities. Troops were billeted in houses throughout the town. Trenches and tank traps were prepared in the parks – the Stray from Zetland Park to Marske, was heavily fortified with several pillboxes. Minefields were sown on the beach, the Stray, and sand dunes. From South Gare to Saltburn and beyond, to the extent of the town boundaries, double-tiered barbed wire was extensively employed.

Redcar High Street with the distinctive town clock and Central cinema. In the foreground can be seen a large emergency static water tank for use in event of bombing, behind which are the public air-raid shelter and gas decontamination centre!

*Left:* The town clock by night with searchlights scanning the Teesside skies for enemy intruders. To the left of the picture can be seen the Regent cinema, only recently opened in 1937.

*Below:* Endless coils of tangled barbed wire isolating the previously closed beaches were a constant, depressing reminder of the possibility of an invasion in 1940. In the early part of January, 300 soldiers were billeted on the racecourse and Marske, with many going to Coatham Convalescent Home and Kirkleatham Hall – other servicemen had to be billeted in guesthouses throughout the town.

The bleak outlook from Granville Terrace along the Stray towards Marske. The concrete cubes in the foreground are anti-tank obstacles, disguised as beach chalets. The seafront buildings are pillboxes. The tower in the far distance is a strong point disguised as a cenotaph, with the Stray as far as Marske consisting of a maze of trench and defence posts, added to which a considerable number of mines had been sown as 1940 progressed.

The River Tees had long been a coastal strongpoint and the village of Warrenby had a barracks for many years to man a coastal gun at the South Gare. The sand dunes opposite Dorman Long steel works was the site of this additional 9.2 Pasley battery coastal gun. Occasional practice firings were carried out throughout the war, notices being given to town residents to open windows to prevent shattering. However the gun was never fired in anger.

Somewhere in the north east, desperate times require desperate measures. This old car filled with concrete needed a farm tractor to pull it into place to act as an effective roadblock in the event of invasion!

With the public mood hitting an all-time low in 1940, the army mounted a morale-boosting nationwide recruiting drive tour, which was warmly welcomed in the towns on Teesside. Here this patriotic crowd gather round AK-AK gun on display on Marton Road, Middlesbrough during the tour, near St John's Church.

*Right:* Nancy Warley (left) and Audrey Jowsey are on the verandah next to the New Pavillion in 1944. These two young ladies didn't let the war dampen their spirits, and found it an exciting time on the social side with many dances. Redcar was flooded with servicemen from the bases in the area. At the many packed dance halls, the girls were never short of a partner, being outnumbered 4-1.

*Below:* Clearly still out of bounds – the west end of the Promenade at the entrance to the boating lake. In the far distance is the indoor swimming bath, which was still open to the public on certain days. The RAF, who were billeted in the nearby Coatham Hotel, used the indoor swimming pool for dinghy training.

Personnel of 80 Wing, RAF Signals' radio station Marske, which consisted of eight wooden buildings with high radio masts, built on land which was part of Horse Close Farm, off Quarry Lane. Wilf Priestnall (back row second from left) was billeted in High Street, Marske, throughout the war and married the daughter of the family. The work these men were engaged in was highly secret, and diverted enemy aircraft away from their target and confused their navigation to return to base.

Noreen Blackburn (second from left in the middle row), went to ATS training camp with wonderful memories of childhood spent in Redcar, the earliest being of days spent on the beach, so many things to see and do! Punch and Judy, roundabouts, and swing boats. Foy boatsman calling 'any more for the Skylark', and on Sundays there was Sunshine corner. The taste of summer, particularly the ice cream from Pacitto's! The rock shop where an old man would fill a little carrier bag with rock goodies, all for 6d! And not forgetting fish and chips from Henderson's, which was in the back alley at Millbank Terrace where Noreen lived. If the sea was too cold for paddling, there was a swimming baths. Saturday morning meant the pictures. There were the Regent, Central and Palace to choose from. The New Pavilion provided live entertainment in the summer: the most famous being Radio Tymes, featuring Billy Breen who went on to become Larry Grayson. Noreen trod the boards of the New 'Pavs', in 1945/6, when the parish players presented *The Blue Bird* and *Peter Pan*. September was magical when the boating lake and Promenade were festooned with twinkling lights. Winter was fun with skating on a frozen Locke Park lake and tobogganing down Black Bridge.

In response to the government's Ministry of Food Campaign to grow more food for the war effort, local schools were working on their own allotments. Volunteers were called for at Coatham Grammar School to spend part of the summer holidays helping on the land. A harvest camp was arranged at Kirlington near Bedale – as can be seen the boys lived under canvas. Although it was hard work, the boys enjoyed the experience and companionship. From left to right, back row: Harland, Readman, Woodruff, Mr Willis (headmaster), Attwood, Buck, Roberts, -?-, Brooks, Sutton, Christensen. Middle row: Burton, Priestley, Hunt, Brodie, Robson, -?-, Burns, Speakman. Front row: Knudson, Smithson, Willis, Currie, Foxton, Robinson, Tait.

Hard at work bringing in the harvest, 1942/3, at Kirklington. Among those seen here are Freddy Ireland, Snowball Robinson, Keith Burns, Christensen, Qualendon.

Access to limited sections of the Redcar beach was permitted in 1943 until 30 September. Hours of opening were 10 a.m. to 12:30 p.m. and 2 p.m. to 5 p.m. Unaccompanied children were not permitted on the beach. Its only access was via the slipway opposite Moore Street – sea bathing and boat trips were prohibited. Nevertheless this young lady was determined to at least get a suntan. It is hard to visualise today just how many huge concrete and barbed wire intrusions were on our once-pleasant holiday town.

A desolate scene of bandstand and shelters, completed in 1905 at a cost of £400, inside the concrete base were toilets. In later years the base was extended to accommodate a semi-circle of shelters, which in the war became ARP posts.

*Above:* A further section of the beach was open for a limited period, which was warmly welcomed by the war-weary Teessiders. The council's 'Holiday At Home' programme in the town was designed to give the workers a short relaxing break away from the daily grind. This beach slipway is opposite Dundas Street, with the ever-present concrete anti-tank blocks and tangled barbed wire. The public were warned about a tarry trench across the sands. However, many did get it on their clothes on a warm day!

*Right:* Five-year-old Ian Denney (left) with friend Barry Johnson, prepared for Hitler's armies in 1940. The photograph was taken at the side of Denney's garage.

The procession of the police and emergency services along Thrush Road, Redcar, passing the rostrum, with the Mayor and other high-ranking military officials taking the salute. The occasion was to attend a memorial service at St Peter's Church, after the death of fifteen prominent Redcar citizens in the air raid when the Zetland Club on Coatham Road was bombed on 21 October 1941. The trees and old stable on the racecourse have now gone to make way for Tesco's supermarket.

Guisborough Westgate, on a damp December morning in 1944, with the official stand-down of the local 1st, 2nd, and 3rd Battalions (Green Howards) Home Guard. On the left are the local police chief, Home Guard commanders and councillors. Not to be left out of it are a contingent of Guisborough children.

Redcar's stand-down parade of the 4th Battalion of Home Guard, probably on the same wet Sunday in December 1944. The cadets presenting arms for the March Past and salute, at Coatham Road Cenotaph. The Mayor (John Spurr Dixon) and Mayoress, with other dignitaries are standing on the right. Just out of the photograph on the left is the open site where the bombed Zetland Club stood.

Elements of Redcar and Guisborough Home Guard out on a weekend exercise at Dibblebridge, near Castleton, East Cleveland. Davison's bakery from Redcar is seen here dishing out meat pasties to a hungry bunch of lads.

By 1943 the Redcar 4th Battalion Home Guard were responsible for the manning of pillboxes on the Stray. This cheerful group of Redcar men, seen here below No. 41 post, Zetland Park, are, from left to right: Mr Kay, Jack Coulthand, Laurie Coultas, and Dougie James holding a Sten gun. The pillbox, like many others, was disguised as a beach chalet!

Large-scale exercises were staged by the East Cleveland Area Home Guard, as seen here in Commondale village. With plenty of smoke and flash bombs they confront an enemy tank. Simulated attacks such as this would eagerly be watched by the locals and certainly livened up the normally quiet country village life. The close proximity of the public house was an essential part of the exercise when the battle was won!

Keen competition and rivalry existed between the different platoons of the Home Guard, especially on the firing range. This photograph, taken on Butt's Lane near Guisborough, shows the range which was in regular use by Redcar and Guisborough subsection, Skelton, Loftus, Saltburn, showing their marksmanship skills with the standard issue 303 Lee-Enfield rifle in 1942.

Instruction on the First World War machine gun on Guisborough range. In the early years of the war very few, if any, of the machine guns could be spared for the Home Guard. It became a welcome addition to the armoury in those desperate times.

# Other titles published by The History Press

## Discovering County Durham and Teesside
CHARLIE EMETT & RON DODSWORTH

Charlie Emett and Ron Dodsworth have chosen 100 of the most fascinating, intriguing and historic sites in County Durham and Teesside – not necessarily the most obvious or well-known tourist traps, but all accessible to the public. From landscape features to obscure villages, from remnants of forgotten industries to surprising buildings, all aspects of the area's history are included here. It is a treat for local residents and an eye-opener for visitors, and will be welcomed by anyone keen to know more about this remarkably varied part of Britain.

978 0 7509 4670 4

## County Durham Strange but True
ROBERT WOODHOUSE

*County Durham Strange but True* illustrates and describes people, places and incidents that are unusual, odd or extraordinary. We discover the truth about flamboyant or eccentric characters, curious buildings, strange place names, weird weather, mazes, standing stones and holes in the ground, unusual customs, local folklore and legend, among many other fascinating items. Robert Woodhouse tells an entertaining story - an alternative history of County Durham that will fascinate residents and visitors alike.

978 0 7509 3731 3

## Billingham
PAUL MENZIES

This fascinating collection of over 200 archive photographs celebrates more than a century of history: beginning in the very earliest days of photography, it moves from the country lanes and farms of the 1920s to the factories and industries of the 1960s and the bustling town of today. Local author Paul Menzies has drawn on interviews with residents for this collection, some conducted as long as thirty years ago. It will delight everyone who knows the town.

978 0 7524 4838 1

## Hartlepool 1946-1997
DOUGLAS R.P. FERRIDAY

This collection of over 200 photographs features Hartlepool people at work, at school, and at play. It shows well-known landmarks like the Empire Theatre, various public buildings, public houses and the profusion of shops that once lined Lynn Street. It also documents many of the changes that have taken place in the docks and how they have affected the lives of local people. Photographs here show Wm Gray's shipyard, coal exporting and timber importing, as well as some of the shipping that used the port.

978 0 7524 0795 1

If you are interested in purchasing other books published by The History Press, or in case you have difficulty finding any History Press books in your local bookshop, you can also place orders directly through our website:

**www.thehistorypress.co.uk**